OXFORD
UNIVERSITY PRESS

E-mails Home

Shilo Berry

To: marvin@keystoke.com new se

Thanks for your e-mail. I am having a great trip. It is fun to travel around the world.

This morning I went for a walk.
I walked for a long time.

To: marvin@keystoke.com

I saw lots of water and I saw lots of big buildings. The buildings were next to the water.

One building was a funny shape.
Do you know where I was?

To: marvin@keystoke.com

I was in Sydney. Sydney is a big city in Australia.

The funny-shaped building I saw was the Sydney Opera House. It was built in 1955.

To: marvin@keystoke.com

new

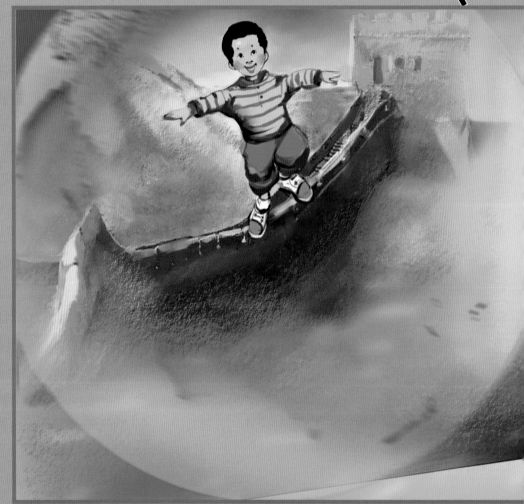

Thanks for your e-mail. I am having a great trip. I have now left Australia.

This morning I went out for another long walk. I walked in the hills.

To: marvin@keystoke.com

new

se

I saw a wall. The wall was high and very wide. The wall was also very long.

People can walk on top of the wall.

No one was there this morning.

Can you guess where I was?

To: marvin@keystoke.com new se▶

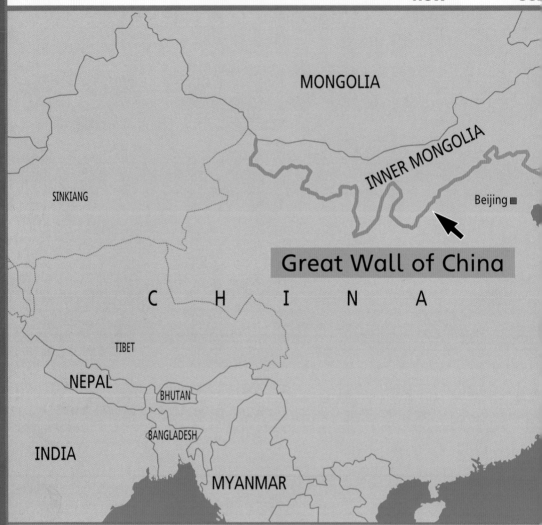

MONGOLIA

INNER MONGOLIA

SINKIANG

Beijing ■

Great Wall of China

C H I N A

TIBET

NEPAL

BHUTAN

BANGLADESH

INDIA

MYANMAR

I was in China. The wall was the
Great Wall of China. It was built
thousands of years ago.

The wall was built to keep China safe from enemies. It is 7,200 km long, but it has fallen down in some places.

To: marvin@keystoke.com

new

Thanks for your e-mail. This trip is great. I have now left China.

This morning I went out again.
I went for another walk. It was
very hot.

To: marvin@keystoke.com
new   se

This morning I saw lots of sand. The sand was orange.

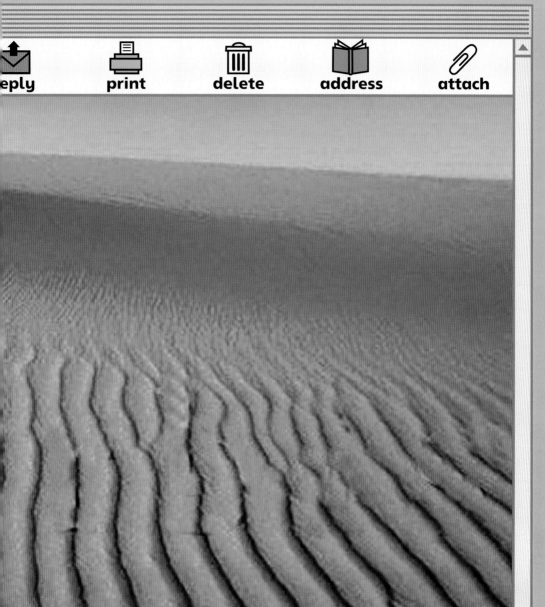

The sand was very hot and dry, and so was I! Do you know where I was? Can you guess?

To: marvin@keystoke.com

new

se

Kalahari Desert

I was in the Kalahari Desert. The Kalahari Desert is in southern Africa.

The Kalahari Desert has many sand dunes. Sand dunes are made when the wind blows the sand into big hills.

To: marvin@keystoke.com
new   se

Thanks for your e-mail. I am having a great trip. I have now left southern Africa.

This morning I went out. I went for a walk. This is the last week of my trip.

To: marvin@keystoke.com

new

se

I saw a palace. There were guards outside the palace. The guards had black trousers and red coats.

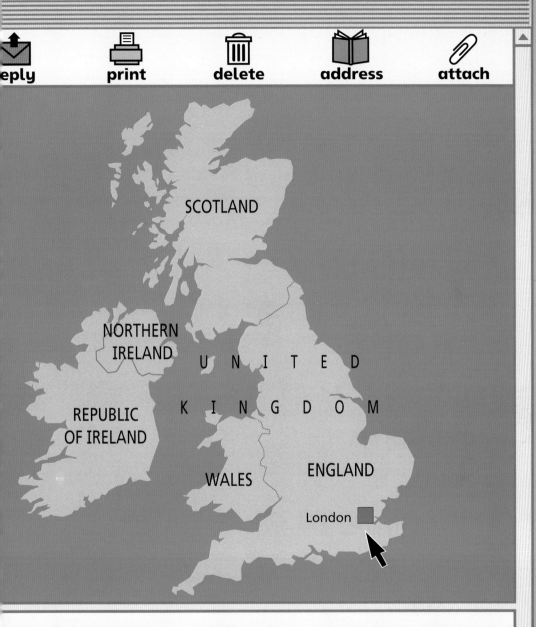

Do you know where I was? I was in London, and London is my home. The palace was Buckingham Palace.

new **send** **reply** **delete** **address** **attach**

Index